IMAGES
of England

WINCHESTER
FROM THE SOLLARS COLLECTION

Winchester College from the air, photographed in early 1997 by Bob Sollar's son, Andrew.

Tempus
Two in One Series

WINCHESTER

Compiled by
John Brimfield and Bob Sollars

TEMPUS

A view of the High Street, 1 June 1962.

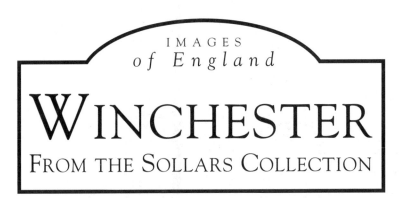

IMAGES
of England

WINCHESTER

FROM THE SOLLARS COLLECTION

Compiled by
John Brimfield

TEMPUS

This edition first published 2001
Copyright © John Brimfield and Bob Sollars, 2001

Tempus Publishing Limited
The Mill, Brimscombe Port,
Stroud, Gloucestershire, GL5 2QG

ISBN 0 7524 2214 6

Typesetting and origination by
Tempus Publishing Limited
Printed in Great Britain by
Midway Clark Printing, Wiltshire

Originally produced as two books:

Winchester from the Sollars Collection
First published 1995
Copyright © John Brimfield, 1995
ISBN 0 7524 0173 4

Around Tring: The Second Selection
First published 1997
Copyright © E.A. (Bob) Sollars, 1997
ISBN 0 7524 1055 5

Contents

Born in Winchester on 25 February 1918, Bob Sollars was educated at Western Infants, Hyde Junior School, and finally St Thomas Senior School where he was elected Head Boy and Captain of football and cricket. A keen footballer, he played three times for Winchester City Schoolboys' Football Team in a national contest. He left school in 1932 and started work in the retail trade.

On the outbreak of war in September 1939 he volunteered for the Royal Navy but went into the Royal Marines. He took part in the Battle of Crete in 1941 but was left behind at the excavation beach on the southern shores of Crete and was captured on 1 June. He spent the rest of the War in Austria, Stalag XVIIIA (Wolfesberg). He at last arrived home in May 1945, and was demobbed in December of the same year.

His interest in photography started at an early age, when with a school friend he experimented with developing and printing under a blanket in the living room of his home. He later started to take photography seriously and joined the Winchester Photographic Society of which he was twice President. During the early 1950s he turned professional, taking over an existing business which traded mostly in local and national press photography, later adding commercial and industrial photography to the business. He retired early in 1990. He is married to Margaret; they have three children, Robert, Andrew, and Roberta, and five grandchildren. Andrew Sollars now runs the business, continuing the 'Sollars of Winchester' photographic tradition, and adding picture framing to his already heavy workload.

Introduction

Living in Winchester has been all the richer thanks to the photographs taken by Mr E.A. (Bob) Sollars over the last few decades. So frequently we see photographs of a life long ago, but Bob Sollars's pictures faithfully record a rapidly changing way of life we all knew and can associate with. Through the good offices of John Brimfield, Mr Sollars has generously made available to a wider audience his magnificent archive – thank goodness he did not throw away his negatives when he retired.

Looking at the pictures, one becomes aware of the subtle and brutal changes that have occurred during the latter part of our second Elizabethan age. Our Victorian forefathers, with the coming of mechanisation, cleared and rebuilt vast areas. Sadly, in most cases, only rudimentary records are available, often broad-sweeping views by Francis Frith or Winchester's own Mr Beloe remain. Our age has seen the enormous pressure on private mobility with living in pleasant suburbs and the need to commute to work. Transport demand has caused the demise of many private businesses and properties. The centre of Winchester is now devoid of living accommodation (although this is coming back) and a whole way of life almost untouched for many centuries has gone for ever. Walking to work now usually means a short trot from the office car park. City centre schools have closed and become car parks as the later twentieth-century person enjoys his own door to door mobility.

Bob Sollars has also captured formal Winchester – the opening of the old Assize Courts with the procession of Judges to the Cathedral before the coming of the new Crown Courts in continual session.

To Wintonians, it is often the background that is of the greatest interest, capturing glimpses of shops that are no more, bus companies such as Greyfriars, King Alfred, and Hants & Dorset that have left our streets, and events we have long forgotten about like rent protests, with, again, shops in the background that were once household names, shops like Lipton's, Timothy Whites, and Taylors, etc. High Street names today change so rapidly that sometimes no record of the frontage has been kept. Yet all is not doom! Thanks to the Winchester Preservation Trust, wiser counsels have prevailed.

Looking at Mr Sollars's picture of my own house it is pleasing to think that the dilapidated street frontage lacking porches, and pale yellow bricks, grubby and painted over, has now been restored to something like its 1840 dignity. There is a realisation that we have limited resources and that the best of the old must be complimented by the late twentieth century. Bob Sollars's pictures have captured the end of the old world and the start of the new.

Finally, we must be grateful to John Brimfield for using his expert knowledge of the City, and realising that the Sollars Collection will appeal to a wider readership as part of the social history of Great Britain. 'Photo Sollars Winchester' will still be in demand many years from now to show the way we lived.

C.J. Webb
Chairman, Winchester Heritage Centre
An enterprise of the Winchester Preservation Trust
30–32 Upper Brook Street, Winchester

One
People

The Judge leaves the Law Courts, housed at the Great Hall, 1 November 1953.

The Fire Station children's Christmas party, held on 19 December 1953.

The Co-op Guild children's party, 9 January 1954.

The Gas Company children's party, 4 January 1954. Leaning on the table is Jill Pollard, opposite are John Pollard and David Bishop.

Hyde Girls Club bell ringers with their instructor, Mr J. King, about to be televised for children's television. This photograph was taken on 5 May 1954.

Hyde School football team with the Revd Williams, June 1954.

The Old Contemptibles service at St Thomas' Church, 11 September 1954.

Father Christmas arrives by helicopter with presents from the U.S. Air Force at the Hampshire depot for the children of the Hampshire County Council homes, 21 December 1954.

Mr Cottrill, the local archaeologist, with a skeleton found during excavations at Winnall building site, 8 January 1955.

The Odeon Cinema road safety campaign, 26 February 1955.

The Odeon Cinema children with their Highway Code books, April 1955.

The retirement of Miss E.F. Sivyour from Holy Trinity School, March 1955.

A diver at Durngate during the construction of the new main sewer from Eastgate Street to the new Winnall Housing Estate, April 1955. On the right is Mr A. Stickland – his hourly rate of pay was two shillings.

Mayor D.M. Edmeades visiting North Walls fire station, demonstrating the fire emergency telephone, 28 April 1955.

Mr Peter Smithers campaigning in the Broadway, May 1955.

Hyde Abbey Ladies' Bowling Club, August 1955.

The Royal Naval Association marching down the High Street to the service of the dedication of the new Standard at St John's Church, 18 September 1955.

A service held for the Royal Hampshire Regiment after their passing out parade in Series House gardens, September 1955.

The Mayor, Mrs B.G. Thackery, visiting the Royal Observer Corps, 18 November 1955.

Winchester Cathedral Bell Ringers being visited by the Mayor and Mr and Mrs Peter Smithers on 13 December 1955.

Marks & Spencer staff Christmas party held on 22 December 1955. Fifth and sixth on the left are Mrs Banning and Mrs Smith. Second from the left, standing at the back, is Mrs Flux.

Old folks' party at Sparsholt village hall, 3 January 1956. Front row: (left to right) Mrs Kimber, Mr Kimber, Mr Maundrel (Vicar), Mr Merwood and Mrs Bayford.

Hants & Dorset bus station children's party in the Guildhall, January 1956.

The boxer Joe Dumper training at
Royal Green Jackets gymnasium
with Mr A. Cozens in March 1956.

The Mayor visiting the Sea Cadet
Corps at training ship *Itchen*,
Parchment Street, 20 March 1956.

Circus elephants arriving at Winchester railway station, 27 June 1956.

West Hill Cricket Club, photographed on 18 August 1956. Front row: (left to right) Mr Ship, Mr Bull and Mr Lucas; on the back row, fifth from left, is Mr Strange.

Wilfred Pickles at the Willow Tree Inn on 14 October 1956, about to push over the column of pennies. Also present is the Mayor, Mr P. Woodhouse.

Brown & Harrisons' Dairy Ltd children's party, 10 January 1957.

An interior view of the West of England Sack Factory at Bar End and some of the staff, 19 February 1957.

Inspection of the St John's Ambulance cadets, 21 March 1957.

Staff of the West of England Sack factory at Bar End Road, now the site of the Hampshire County Council supplies depot, photographed on 10 April 1957.

Mr Charles Mann, the City of Winchester mace bearer, photographed on 10 July 1957.

Brown and Harrisons' Dairy children's Christmas party, 1 January 1958.

The Post Office children's Christmas party, 4 January 1958.

The Police receive their new badge and helmet, March 1958.

After being presented with their new badge and helmet in March, the Police received a new mode of transport, on 18 December 1958.

County High School prefects, 4 June 1958.

Mr W. Goodchild, street cleaner, at work in North Walls on 4 February 1960. Note the two-way traffic before the coming of the one-way system.

The staff of Mortons' Glass Works in St Swithun Street, working on a stained glass leaded window, 12 May 1960.

The 'Penguins' swimming gala at the Lido, 21 July 1960.

The Army Cadet Force in Middle Brook Street central car park, September 1960. The building on the left was Harman & Co., the rag and bone store.

All Saints' School football team
with Mr Lewington (on the left),
March 1961.

An interior view of Worthy Down
signal box, 28 October 1961.

The collection point for the Mile of Pennies outside St Peter's Church, December 1962.

Staff being collected for the Brown and Harrison's Dairy staff outing at the Cart and Horses Inn, Kingsworthy, in May 1963.

In May 1964, a protest against hanging took place outside Winchester Prison. Note the old pedestrian entrance opposite St James Lane.

The Ballards of Winnall football team as it was in May 1964. Back row: (from third left) Mr Tracey, Mr Pink, Mr Budgen, and Mr Whitcher. In the front row on the left is Mr Ballard; also pictured are Mr Dumper, Mr Foulds, Mr Carter, and Mr Ivory.

Mrs M. Palmer receiving a cheque from a bingo caller in August 1964. From left to right: Mr M. Fletcher, Mrs D. Smith, and Ritz manager Mr J. Pitt.

Mr A. Phillis, a watch and clock maker, attending to the clock at Lloyds Bank, September 1964.

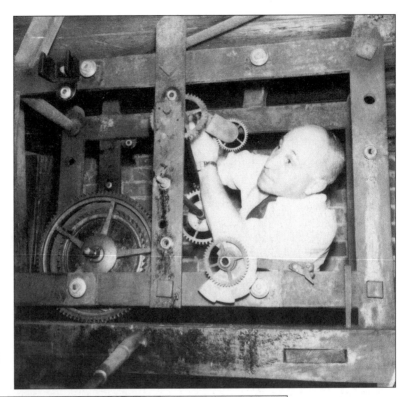

Mr Phillis working on the clock mechanism.

Mr L.G.L. Chew, the City Champion, receives a savings challenge from the Mayor of Salisbury, Councillor W.S. Biddle, on behalf of the Mayor of Winchester, Mrs B. Carpenter Turner, in October 1966.

The Winchester and District Cub Scouts marching on the St George's Day parade, 28 April 1968.

Field Marshal Lord Montgomery of Alamein addressing pupils after the official renaming of the school, June 1968.

These members of King Alfred Boys' Club are 'kidnapping' Mr Ken Wapshire, the proprietor of Ken's Fish and Chip Shop (26 October 1968).

The Mayor, Alderman S.G. Steel, proclaims the dissolution of Parliament from the steps of the City Cross, May 1970.

Mr Abrahams,
manager of the Lido
swimming pool,
pictured in
September 1971.

The last sessions of
the Magistrates'
Court in the
Guildhall, February
1972.

A protest
march held by
Winchester
tenants against
rent increases,
May 1972.

Pickets in the High Street, September 1972. These workmen, employed on the construction of the new Law Courts, were on strike for a guaranteed weekly wage of £30. In view on the right is the Old Holm Oak Tree.

One of the hobbies on display in an exhibition held at the Guildhall in December 1972, with the Mayor and Mr Foot of the Rotary Club and Mr W. Eyles.

The firemen's strike of May 1977. These pickets are outside the Hampshire County Council offices in Romsey Road.

The Mayor, Mr David G. Ball, holds a party under the Pentice for Winchester old age pensioners to commemorate the Queen's Silver Jubilee in June 1977.

Sign-writer Mr Thompson re-writes the names of Winchester's parliamentary representatives on the wall of the Great Hall.

A memorial to Mr Douglas Bylett in the High Street, outside Lloyds Bank. This was removed on Sunday 18 May 1980, soon after this picture was taken.

Two
Transport

The Hampshire County Council's first mobile library van was a specially designed Bedford built to carry 1850 books. It was officially opened by Sir Charles Chute, Bart., M.C., Chairman of Hampshire County Council, in July 1953.

This accident at Stockbridge Road railway bridge took place on 3 June 1954.

An Anglo-American vintage car rally passes through the city, 10 September 1954.

Moorside Motor Works in Union Street, August 1955.

The showrooms of Wessex Motors in St Cross Road, April 1956.

The Winchester by-pass photographed on 30 April 1958. Also in the view is Spitfire Bridge.

Mr R. Johnson, fruit and vegetable merchant of Lower Brook Street, photographed on 12 July 1958.

46

A 'Red Rover' stage coach at the India Arms on 9 September 1958.

The new Bull Bros motor workshop at Winnall (late of Cossack Lane), 19 December 1958. After this, their old premises were occupied by T.A. Hutchinson, builder.

A fleet of new cars for Richardson & Starling Ltd of Hyde Street, 1 January 1959.

An accident at Weeke Pond, 9 January 1959. Note the old Police box on the left.

Mr H.L. Bradley's garage in Staple Gardens, May 1961.

Mr Charles Salter's new 'Caterer's' van seen in Eastgate Street in February 1962.

A view of the central car park, now the Brooks Centre, 1 June 1962.

The entrance to the central car park and a row of four shops on the right-hand side, June 1962.

An accident near Whitchurch involving a King Alfred bus, which took place in December 1962.

An accident in St John's Street, September 1964.

A Camill dumper manufactured by Campbell & McGill Engineering of Winnall, April 1965.

Another accident involving a King Alfred bus, this time at the junction of Chilbolton Avenue and Stockbridge Road, April 1965. This bus, which spent some time in America, was recently purchased and returned to Winchester.

Part of the Will Short Ltd garage showrooms in St Cross Road, May 1965. Note, on the right-hand side, the start of the demolition of Hooper & Ashby Ltd, builders' merchants.

H.J. Coombes & Co. Ltd of Andover Road, May 1965.

The Market Service Station, Andover Road, May 1965.

A large load travelling north on the south-bound lane of the by-pass after leaving the Petersfield Road. October 1966.

The same large load crossing over to the north-bound lane at Winnall cross roads, by Wadham's Garage.

A general view of the High Street as it looked in August 1967. Then, traffic used to enter the High Street from Little Minster Street.

The Airlie Road corner in December 1968, with Winchester City Association Football Club ground. The Club was founded in 1884.

The official opening of the Bar End flyover in August 1973. The ceremony was performed by the Mayoress, Mrs C.A. Taylor.

The Bar End junction, August 1973. Note the police and contractors ready to close the central reservation and Morstead Road.

Weekes Garage/Lewtas Motors. The price of petrol was 72p and 74p a gallon. July 1978.

A motor cycle demonstration in the city in March 1979. The demonstrators were protesting against the wearing of crash helmets. They are seen here entering Andover Road.

Three
Buildings

During excavations on the corner of Middle Brook Street and St George's Street, a Roman mosaic was found. This picture was taken on 1 September 1953.

This picture, dated 14 November 1953, shows the high price of new laid eggs, 5s. 6d. or 5s. 9d. a dozen – for some, nearly twice the hourly rate of pay!

A snow scene in Sussex Street (City Road end), January 1954.

The junction of Chesil Street and Bridge Street, January 1954. The end building in Bridge Street is Ken's Fish and Chip Shop before it moved to its new location on the corner of St John's Street.

Winnall Industrial Estate, showing Curtis & Padwick, 6 August 1954.

Westcombe Motors pictured on 1 December 1954 after it had collapsed in City Road. Behind the trees is the Hermit's Tower.

Union Street from North Walls on 22 February 1955. The buildings on the right of the picture have since all been demolished. Note the metal dustbins!

The interior of Ponsford's Bakery in North Walls as it appeared in February 1955.

The Co-op bakery and staff, February 1955. Pictured are: (left to right) Mr Mumford, Mr Mumford, Mr Shepherd, Mr Saunders, Mr Habgood, and Mr Dillow.

The demolition of houses in North Walls, 28 April 1955.

The Post Office Tavern in Parchment Street, 27 November 1955. On the right is J. Stone, gents' hairdressers.

The mayor visiting R.H.C.H. hut wards during Christmas 1955.

The St George & The Dragon leaded light above the front entrance door to the George Hotel, March 1956.

The St George's
Street and Jewry
Street corner
during demolition,
15 March 1956.

The top of St
George's Street,
15 March 1956.
The first building
on the left is
Kingdons. Also in
the picture is the
City Tavern. Note
the pedestrian
walkway from the
garage to the
hotel.

An interior view of the Cadena Cafe (now the Baker's Oven), photographed on 14 November 1956.

The Queen's Head, Upper Brook Street, 20 June 1957.

Will Short's Ltd, Southgate Street, 11 September 1957. The white house was later demolished. The building next door is Crosby's sports shop.

Father Christmas arriving in a 1903 Humber at Sherriff and Ward on 23 November 1953.

Morris dancers in Castle Yard, 21 July 1958.

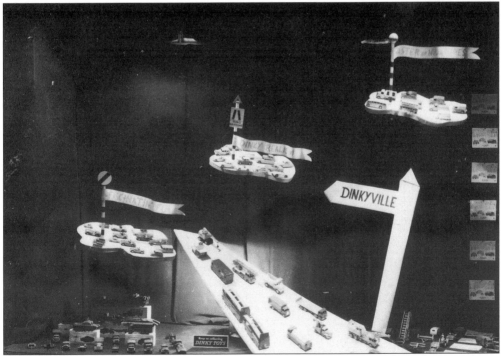

Hollands' shop window in the Upper High Street showing a display of Dinky toys, pictured on 21 July 1958.

The south corner of Colebrook Street looking from the Cathedral, 10 October 1958. At the top, in the centre, is the playground of St Mary's School.

A display of Brazil's pies, 21 January 1959, in Hubert Smith's shop in the City Road. The pies cost 2s. 8d. and 3s. each.

The demolition of the gasometer in Andover Road, 20 March 1959. The gasometer had been constructed in 1856. Gas lighting was introduced to the High Street in 1832, and in 1834 it was extended to the whole city.

The interior of Mr S. Offord's shop at 77 North Walls, opposite Hyde Abbey Road. The date is 1 May 1959, Rowntree's fruit gums cost 3d., Cadbury's Roses 1s. 1d. per quarter, and Nutty Nutty sweets are 7d. per quarter.

The new Hampshire County Council offices, 11 May 1959.

The K.R.R.C. advertising a film at the Odeon on 15 May 1959.

The B.P. drilling rig at Chilcombe, 14 November 1959. The rig was test drilling to assess the possibility of gas storage underground over an area of 3500 acres.

Woolford & Sons, builders, at Bar End Road, November 1959.

Hyde Street looking south, March 1960, and (below) looking north.

In this picture dating from March 1960 we are looking at the Post Office Engineers entrance and Hyde Abbey Motor Works. The houses in the foreground were demolished to make way for petrol pumps and car showrooms.

The entrance to Hyde Abbey Motors showing workshops and petrol pumps, March 1960.

Do you remember the High Street as it looked in 1960? This and the following set of seventeen pictures were all taken on the same day, 25 July 1960. Shown here is Plummers.

Hepworth's.

Heming & Tudor.

Allen's.

Liptons.

T. Walton.

Burtons.

Hayter's.

Dowlings.

Wymans.

John Collier.

New Bell & Crown.

Currys.

Home & Colonial.

Dunn's.

Sherriff & Ward's.

Hutchins.

Churchill's.

Pictured here in July 1960, the Mercantile Store's last day of trading was 17 September of that year.

Luck's the chemist in Southgate Street. The date is 29 September 1960, and Miss Dorothy Gain is receiving her £100 prize from the Sebbix Shampoo manager. On the left is Mr E. Luck.

Trod Smith's building being converted into Jaeger's, 25 October 1960. On the right is the Wimpy Bar.

The Awdry Tea Rooms which used to be above W.H. Smith & Sons in the High Street. This was one of only six Awdry tea rooms; the other five were in Bournemouth, Darlington, Durham, Brussels, and Paris.

The interior of Hutchins sweet shop, May 1960. This now forms part of the Blue Dolphin Fish Restaurant.

The Mayor of Winchester, Councillor Lt Col. D.C. Spelman, who officially opened the Old Chesil Rectory after it had undergone extensive renovations. With the Mayor is Councillor Stanley Steel. (19 May 1961).

The arrival of the Bishop of Winchester, Dr A.T.P. Williams, for the dedication of St Luke's Church on 12 July 1961.

The Square as it looked on 16 September 1961. E.J. Hibberd was the last umbrella repair shop in the city.

The Square, 16 September 1961.

The Bull Drove swimming pool in Garnier Road in 1961. The caretaker at that time was Mr Ted Wilkins.

Pearson's salerooms in Tower Road (the five corners), 11 December 1961.

After a lightning strike on the gable end of a house in Canute Road, January 1962.

The Mercantile Stores under demolition. The last day trading was 17 September 1960. This photograph was taken in February 1962.

The foundations of the Wessex Hotel, built by Drewitts, pictured on 1 June 1962.

Boundary Street looking towards Eastgate Street, August 1963. Numbers 1–7 are still standing.

Boundary Street looking looking west. On the right-hand is Tagart, Morgan and Coles, timber importers, August 1963.

Friarsgate looking east in June 1964. The Greyfriars flats are under construction.

Friarsgate looking towards the central car park, June 1964

Hancock's staff and their vans. This picture was taken on 19 December 1964 in Park Avenue on the parade ground of the A.T.C. Third from the left is Mr Hayward; next is Mr Pickett; and last in the line, on the right, is Mr Burgess.

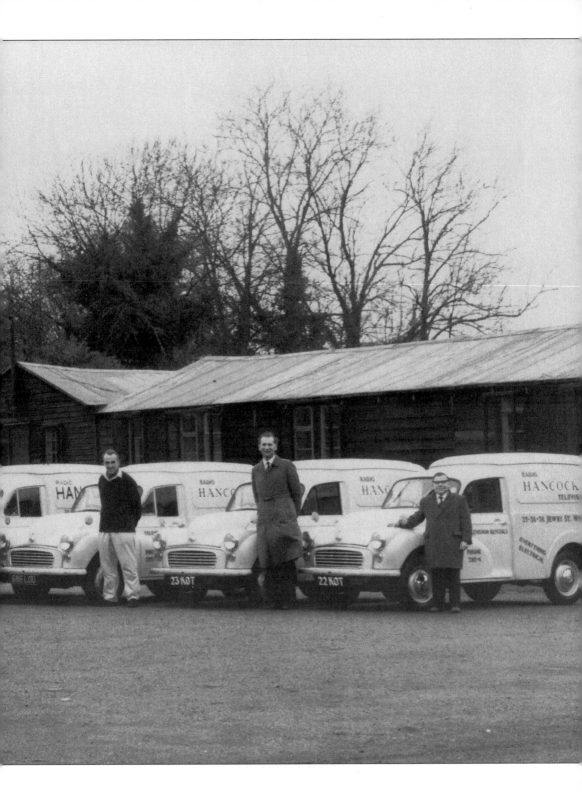

A fire above the Theatre Royal bar on 20 January 1965.

The remains of the old Law Courts as they looked in March 1965. The Law Courts had been demolished in 1937 due to subsidence.

The Goodyear Tyre Co. in Victoria Road.

Weapons in the cells of North Walls police station, handed in during a firearms amnesty in November 1965.

A Round Table bonfire night procession through the Broadway, November 1965.

Tower Street, January 1966. On the left is the construction site of the multi-storey car park.

The corner of Jewry Street, January 1966.

The fire at Teague and King's, 18 Little Minster Street, which struck in February 1966.

H.R.H. Princess Margaret opened the new Police Headquarters in October 1966. Here we see the March Past by the Special Constables.

The Old Blue Boar Inn, hit by a gib of Caswell Cranes of Winnall, October 1966.

Edwin Carter's, builders, loading up the new bank counter top, October 1966.

The counter top going into Portsmouth Trustee Savings Bank on the Jewry Street/St George's Street corner.

A tank in the Broadway in April 1967. On the right-hand side is the King Alfred snack bar.

Dick's on the Silver Hill/Cross Keys Passage corner. This is now Hunts the Chemist. December 1967.

The Abbey gardens as they looked on 6 March 1968.

Lower Moors Road on the Winnall Industrial Estate in April 1968.

Southgate Street, 27
June 1968.

Andover Road Cattle
Market, August 1968.

A fire at the Guildhall on 28 April 1969. Note the holes in the firemen's hose!

Winton Court Hotel, Southgate Street, pictured in October 1969.

The interior of the Georgian Restaurant in Jewry Street in November 1969.

Rivers Engineering Co., Winnall, March 1970.

The old G.P.O. sorting desk, April 1970.

The new Council Offices under construction in Colebrook Street, January 1970.

The opening of the new Council Offices by the Mayor, July 1970.

St Cross Road showing Newton's Nurseries on the left, September 1972.

The old Market Inn and G.H. Bell, September 1972.

The Castle Hotel, October 1972.

Post Office Telephone Engineers, 75 Hyde Street, January 1973.

The Odeon Cinema,
February 1973.

Lord Hailsham
opening the
new Law
Courts, 22
February 1974.

The Georgian Restaurant in Jewry Street, June 1973.

North Walls shops, October 1974.

The north side of City Road (above) and the south side (below), August 1975.

The view up Andover Road, August 1975.

The corner of Sussex Street in August 1975, before road widening.

Mr Mike Shannon
of Southampton
and England
football teams,
opening Milletts'
new shop in
September 1975.

Chesil Street
looking from East
Hill corner in
September 1975.

River cleaning in the park, with the classrooms of Danemark School in view in the background. October 1975.

Jewry Street in October 1978.

The last of Colson Road in July 1980.

The Theatre Royal in August 1981, before redecoration.

Four
Cathedral and Close

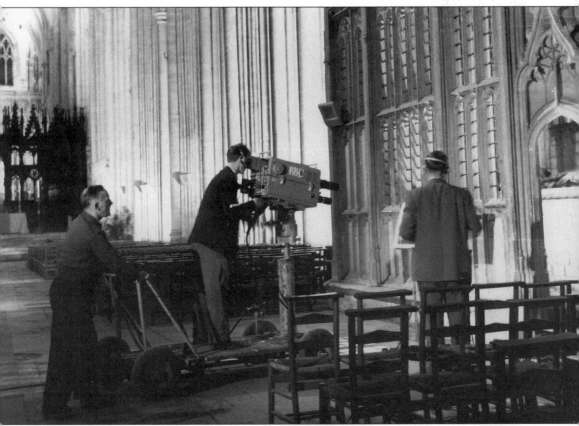

A television camera in action, broadcasting from the Cathedral on 26 November 1954. The Dean of Winchester, The Very Revd Dr E.G. Selwyn, gave the commentary. The programme was also broadcast to viewers in France.

The Judges' Sunday procession to the Cathedral, 13 May 1955.

The Hampshire Carabiniers Yeomanry Guidon in Winchester Cathedral on Sunday morning 6 November 1955, prior to it being laid up. Either side of Sir Dymoke White, the Honorary Colonel, are Colonel J.F.N. Baxendale, Lieutenant-Colonel J.P. Purvis, and Major A.K. Freeman. With the standard is Captain P.W. Ryan, and his escorts are B.S.M. Pearce and B.S.M. Brimfield.

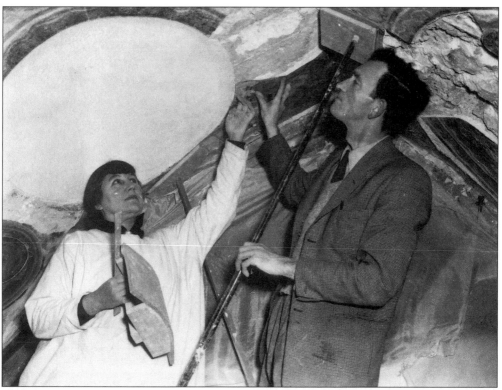

Restoration work under the vault of the Guardian Angel Chapel, 31 December 1957. The work was carried out by Professor and Mrs R.W. Baker of the Royal College of Art.

View from the South Side, 27 September 1964.

Cathedral pillars under repair, January 1965.

Excavations on the North Side of the Cathedral, October 1965.

The Archbishop of Canterbury, The Most Revd Michael Ramsey, blessing the congregation from the Shrine of St Swithun at the Patronal Festival in the Cathedral, which took place in July 1966. The congregation numbered three thousand.

The Vienna Boys' Choir photographed in Winchester Cathedral, March 1971.

The Judges drive to court in horse and carriage (1974).

The enthronement of a new Bishop of Winchester, The Rt Revd John Taylor, on 8 February 1975. Pictured are: (left to right) The Dean of Winchester, The Very Revd Michael Stancliffe; The Archbishop of Canterbury, The Most Revd Donald Coggan; and The Bishop of Winchester.

126

The restoration of Pilgrims Hall, in a photograph taken on 3 March 1959. In the centre at the front is Mr J. Bass, and on the right at the front is Mr A. Trueman, the general foreman.

This medieval dinner was held in Pilgrims Hall in November 1969 in aid of the Cancer Relief Fund. Note the timber frame of the Hall.

The St Cross Dole, the porter to the Lodge, Mr E.A. Sollars, and a visitor. September 1969.

Acknowledgements

The author would like to thank the following people and organisations for their help with the compilation of the book, which is, above all, an endeavour to stir memories of the not too distant past for the reader.

First and foremost, thanks to Mr E.A. (Bob) Sollars for allowing access to the remaining stock of nearly 20,000 sets of negatives from where all the pictures in this publication come. They all carry the credit line 'Photo Sollars Winchester'. Also to the darkroom technician Mr L. Mears, who has printed all the negatives in this book, and the Wintonians who have helped with the information – Mr A. Stickland, Mr A. Brown, Mr A. Brooks, Mr C. Webb, Mr B. Whitcher, Mr J. Hyde, Mrs D. Thompson, and Mr L. Miles. To the Hampshire County Library, especially Mrs P. Stevens and the staff of the Local Studies Department for their help with the *Hampshire Chronicle* files and the loan of fifteen negatives from their collection of photographs from the Sollars Collection. Thanks also to the Curator of Winchester Cathedral.
I would like to offer a tribute also to my wife, Jennifer, for her endless patience and co-operation over the last two years; and to my sons, Robert, with his typing skills, and Julian, for his help with the computer programming.
And not forgetting the Winchester Heritage Centre, where in time there will be an even greater collection of photographs thanks to Bob Sollars.

IMAGES
of England

WINCHESTER
A SECOND SELECTION

Compiled by
E.A. (Bob) Sollars

TEMPUS

First published 1997
Copyright © E.A. (Bob) Sollars, 1997

The Chalford Publishing Company
St Mary's Mill, Chalford,
Stroud, Gloucestershire, GL6 8NX

ISBN 0 7524 1055 5

Typesetting and origination by
The Chalford Publishing Company
Printed in Great Britain by
Bailey Print, Dursley, Gloucestershire

*Cover illustration. St Paul's church choir with, in the centre, Revd B.S. de Witt-Batty MA,
Vicar of St Paul's and left, Revd David Apps with choir master Keith Pearce,
taken outside the church in the early 1960s.*

The Queen receives a bouquet from Jenette Emery-Wallis on her arrival at the Castle
Winchester after attending the Maundy Service in the Cathedral in 1979. On the left is Mr
Lynton White, chairman of Hampshire County Council and on the right is Mr Keith Robinson,
chief executive.

Contents

Acknowledgements

My negatives have for some time been placed in permanant care in several establishments in the city. The creation of this second selection of local photographs in the Archive Photographs Series meant that some 500 negatives were retrieved from these sources to select and print about 250 photographs. I would therefore like to thank the Winchester Museum Service, the Heritage Centre and Winchester Library for their efforts in returning the negatives to me. I further thank John Brimfield who, with his experience in compiling *Winchester from the Sollars Collection* in the Archive Photographs Series, has been a keen supporter when I have needed it. He has spent many a morning with me which has speeded up the completion of this second volume in the same series. Thanks to my wife Margaret for her support and the constant supply of coffee. My thanks also to those people whom I have phoned and who have given me information regarding names and the dates of some photographs which had not been recorded; to Mary Short, Dora Cooke, Len Bumstead and, finally, to Ray Helliwell, for his help in finishing the book.

E.A. (Bob) Sollars
Winchester 1997

Foreword

Standing on Winchester's Westgate and looking over the narrow streets which run down the hill to the River Itchen, the place where much of England's history has been made lies before one's eyes. From the earliest days of England's records this thoroughfare has been trodden by people, royal, political, ecclesiastical, industrial and ordinary, around whom the history of this country is built. Yet today there is little about the street to suggest its age or importance. Scraps of old buildings are to be seen here and there, but the Georgian destroyers did their work well.

In this second selection of photographs taken by E.A. (Bob) Sollars, together with the first volume, *Winchester from the Sollars Collection*, a unique picture of the city is represented during the years from 1946 to the late 1980s, as well as one or two images which were taken in the 1930s and the even earlier school photograph at Hyde which was taken by 'A.N. Other'. Bob remembers most of the names of his class mates after all these years. It will be noticed that a few subjects in the High Street are similar to a few of the images in the first volume; they have been included to show, individually, the old, well known shops in the Pentice area - the type of shop which has been forced out by the larger superstores around Winchester. This of course, regrettably, is a sign of the times.

The changes which have occurred during these years will perhaps attract interest not only because of demolition and the construction of new buildings, which are not as interesting as some they replace, but because of the volume of traffic we now have to endure after the comparative quiet of the 1950s and '60s when it was easy to travel in and out of Winchester, going out of town on the same street on which you arrived, with the traffic travelling both ways - even in the High Street. The only one way system was through Westgate, going up and down for just a few yards. St Georges Street was a little difficult in both directions in the 1950s, as was Jewry Street before the demolition of the George Hotel. Oh yes! There were no traffic wardens; you could park almost anywhere, but of course folk used their feet a lot more than they do today - pleasant memories?

So gaze upon the past and reflect in your mind if you would prefer those 'good old days', or the hustle and bustle of today.

View overlooking the city of Winchester from St Giles' Hill, showing the High Street snaking up through the centre of the picture.

One
High Street

View through the Westgate looking down the High Street with St Giles' Hill in the background, 1965.

A view of the upper High Street during the building of the new Hampshire County Offices, Queen Elizabeth Court, in 1956.

The Westgate, closed for repairs in 1955.

The underground passageway beneath the castle yard is one of only a few which lead to various parts of the city centre, shown here in October 1963.

The top of the High Street after road alterations in 1961.

11

Westgate Lodge Hotel, High Street, in 1961.

Basticks' men's and ladies' outfitters in 1958.

One of three wall paintings on
the stairway of Basticks in 1958.

Cutting down the Holm Oak in the High Street, 1980.

Looking down St Clements Street in 1968.

Cellars in St Clements Street were used as air raid shelters during the Second World War. This one was photographed in 1967.

Clearing the sight for the new Law Courts in Castle Yard in 1966.

Staple Gardens in 1965 showing Warren's and Hodder's rear entrances; further along the road is the Staple Inn, originally the New Inn.

The Westminster Bank and the Jaeger shop on the corner of Jewry Street and the High Street in 1964.

Junction of High Street with Jewry Street in 1965.

16

The High Street, with the
George Hotel still standing,
shown here in 1955.

The Dolphin Inn on the corner
of the High Street and St
Thomas Street, 1981.

Lloyds Bank and the High Street clock in 1968. The Curfew Bell is still housed here and rings at 8.00 pm every day.

Looking up the High Street from the Butter Cross in 1969.

Shops in the High Street opposite the Pentice in 1969.

Parchment Street viewed from the High Street in 1961.

Shops along the Pentice, looking up the High Street, 1963.

Bishop Brothers' shoe shop, the Pentice, 1963.

20

Burton's men's tailors, looking from Parchment Street in 1963.

Baker's hardware and tool shop, the Pentice, 1963.

Hayter's china and glassware, the Pentice, 1963.

The Cadena Cafe, the Pentice, 1963.

22

The Fifty Shilling Tailors,
1963.

R.G. Gifford, corn and coal
merchants, c. 1964.

International Stores
opposite Market
Street, 1968.

Dowlings the draper, 1968.

The lower half of the High Street looking towards St Giles' Hill in 1967.

Sydney man's shop and Russell & Bromley, 1964.

The Home & Colonial store, 1958.

Bridge Street by City Mill, with a view up to the Broadway in 1977. The old Great Western Hotel is evident in the foreground on the left.

Churchill's paper shop next to
Cross Keys Passage, 1967.

Sherriff & Ward's store,
opposite Middle Brook Street,
was one of the major shops in
Winchester High Street in
1961 when this photograph
was taken.

Abbey House from the Abbey grounds, with a view of the statue of King Alfred in 1965.

A fine view of the Broadway from the tower of St John's South in 1972.

Two

Cathedral

A view of the west end of Winchester Cathedral after the old trees had been removed and replanted with younger ones, *c.* 1985.

A crowded Cathedral for the memorial service to Sir Winston Churchill in 1965.

Red Cross Cadets entering the Cathedral for a service in April 1966.

30

Clergy and choir parading from the castle to the Cathedral for the 1979 Palm Sunday service.

Members of the Merchant Navy parade in the Close before entering the Cathedral for the Annual Shipping Festival service on 24 June 1959.

Mr Henry Viney and his assistant, Ray Merwood, cleaning the woodwork from the Cathedral choir stalls in his workshop in Chesil Street, *c*. 1968.

Miss Lydia Kirk, the first lady stone mason to be employed by the Cathedral, is seen here in March 1980 working on a replacement stone block during the constant repairs to the fabric of the Cathedral.

This wood carving of a choir boy on one of the stalls in the Lady Chapel looks, some say, remarkably like *Beatle* Paul McCartney.

The crypt of the Cathedral which floods after heavy rain. Norman Gooding, the Cathedral stone mason, sits on the wellhead in February 1968.

Field Marshall Lord Montgomery of Alemein was a visitor to the Cathedral in September 1968. He is seen here in the centre with, from left to right, Steve Blake (clerk of works), Norman Gooding (stone mason), Bill Collison and the Dean of Winchester the Very Revd O.H. Gibbs-Smith.

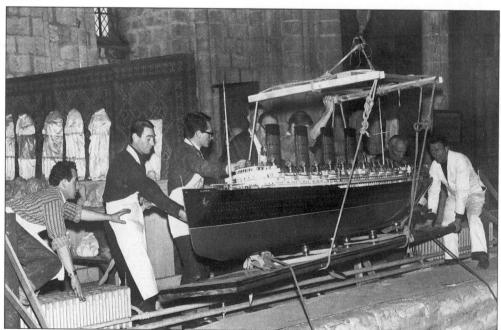

Workmen removing the model of the *Mauritania* in 1966, which had been in the Cathedral for many years. It was rehoused in the Maritime Museum in Southampton.

Staff and members of the congregation after a service in the Cathedral, seen here in the dean's garden with the Archbishop of Canterbury, Dr Donald Coggan and the Bishop of Winchester, the Right Revd J. Taylor.

A group of Cathedral bell ringers photographed in the Cathedral Close in 1959.

Descendants of William Walker, the diver who worked underwater to shore up the sinking south side of the Cathedral from 1905 to 1912, being interviewed by Mr A.P. Whitaker, the city archivist in June 1972. On the right is Winchester sculptor Mr Norman Pierce, who created a model of the diver.

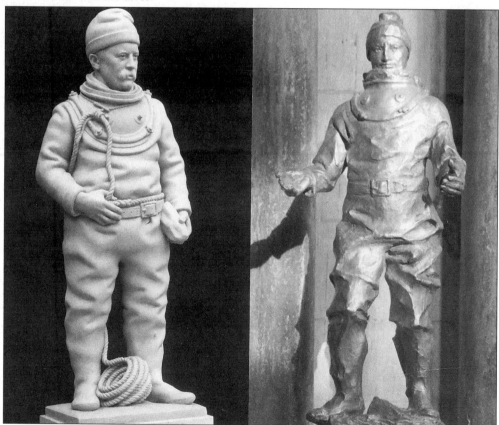

On the left is the life-like model of William Walker, created by Norman Pierce and on the right, the model of William Walker installed in the Cathedral and created by Sir Charles Wheeler, President of the Royal Academy at the time.

Winchester Cathedral Choir practise with organist and choir master Mr Martin Neary.

The one and only fire fighting appliance the Cathedral had in the early days, shown here in 1966, is now in the City Fire Station Museum at North Walls.

The mayor, Mrs Barbara Carpenter Turner, explains the history of the black font to visitors in 1966, with Alan Blake the head verger on the left. This font is one of only a very few in the same style in Britain; there are others in St Mary Bourne church, St Michael's in Southampton, East Meon, Lincoln Cathedral and St Peter's, Ipswich.

STUDY TO BE QUIET

The Izaak Walton window in the south transept of the Cathedral, entitled 'Study to be Quiet'. Full details about this window and the Cathedral can be found in Canon Fred Bussby's book *Winchester Cathedral 1079-1979*.

Three

People

Members of the ambulance service angling club with their catch after a successful day sea fishing in May 1965.

The President of the Hampshire Red Cross Society, Dorothy Countess of Malmesbury, receiving a Bon Homme Bus at the county headquarters in Weeke, with Miss E.M. Balfour and staff in April 1966.

A group of Winchester residents protesting at rent rises outside the Guildhall in September 1972.

The St Johns Ambulance Brigade receive a new vehicle from members of the Winchester Round Table in June 1972.

Members of the Twyford Company of Girl Guides after the St George's Day Parade service in the Cathedral in 1957.

Scouts and Cubs march past the Guildhall where the Mayor of Winchester, Councillor C.H. Bones, takes the salute at the St George's Day Parade in April 1966.

Some of the members of the Scout's Gang Show at the Guildhall in February 1966.

Twyford church bell ringers, October 1974.

Stanmore School pupils who held a May Fair at the school in May 1956.

Just one of the floats that took part in the Weeke Gymkhana in July 1956.

Sutton Scotney Carnival Queen and her attendants in June 1958.

Jack Warner was famous for his part in the popular BBC series *Dixon of Dock Green*. Here he opens the fete at the Garrison sports field, Bar End, in June 1959.

Another float, this time in the Fair Oak Carnival in August 1955.

Kings Somborne football team, December 1958.

The Conder football team in 1958.

Hyde football team, May 1959.

Highcliffe Corinthians at the Lido with a recently won trophy in 1956.

Eastgate cricket team, July 1957.

The YMCA cricket team, August 1956.

Hyde Ramblers cricket team, July 1958.

The Castle cricket team in June 1956.

49

Members of the Friary Bowling Club in 1970.

Lord Bob Boothby bowling at the 1956 Kings Worthy Conservative Fete, with Mrs Peter Smithers and Mr Harry Mills looking on.

Headmaster Dr Freeman receives a seat from Peter Symonds Old Boys Association in 1956.

The Mayor of Winchester, Mrs F.S. Thackeray, with members of the Winchester and District Rotary Club in the Abbey grounds after the presentation of the seat to the city in May 1956.

The mayor, Councillor Miss Evelyn Barnes, receiving a gift of a Civic Sword from Councillors Eric and Dilys Neate to commemorate their combined services as councillors to the city in 1957.

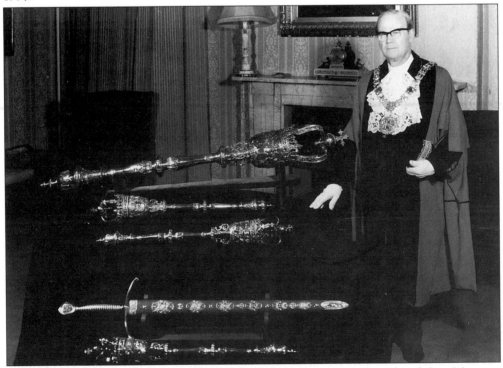

The mayor, Councillor Stanley Steel photographed with the Civic Sword and City Maces in Abbey House in 1970. The four maces were made by Benjamin Pyne of London in 1722-23. The largest mace, together with that of the City of London which is the same size, are probably the two largest civic maces in the country.

The mayor, Councillor Stanley Steel, with judges in the Cathedral Close in November 1964. Also in the picture are Councillor Mrs D. Richards, Mr Robin McCall (town clerk) and Major A.K. Freeman.

The Bishop of Southampton the Right Revd K.E.N. Lamplugh after the dedication service at the opening of the new junior school at St Swithuns in 1966. Also in the group are Mr R. Sawyer (architect), Miss P.M.C. Evans MA (headmistress), Mrs B. Carpenter-Turner and Miss M. Wells.

The war memorial at Shawford Down. The fine view of Twyford and beyond makes a superb setting for a group photograph of these walkers in 1965.

The mayor, Councillor Miss E. Barnes, with senior citizens outside Abbey House before setting off for a trip to Swanage in 1958.

Members and friends of King Alfred Boys Club set off for a sponsored walk in 1963.

A hot summer's day was the cause of this queue outside the Lido swimming pool in Worthy Lane, June 1965.

Skaters enjoy the rare occurrence of Winnall Moors freezing over in the winter of 1956.

More Winchester folk enjoy skating - and spectating - at Winnall Moors in January 1956.

Two local lads enjoy the flooded Garrison playing fields at Bar End in 1960, but not for long...

... Soon after firemen began pumping water from the flooded field.

The machine which printed the *Hampshire Observer* weekly newspaper at Warrens in the High Street. Ken Lee gives the machine a little maintenance.

Compositors Bert Mason, Ernie Beadle, Keith Burrows and Dave Murray in 1957.

Hard at work making up the pages of the *Hampshire Observer* are Jim Elsworthy and Percy Whetton in March 1957.

The staff of the weekly county newspaper the *Hampshire Chronicle* at the Odeon cinema in 1959.

The telephone exchange as it was in 1956, before it was renovated.

Miss Dora Cooke, officer in charge of the Winchester exchange, explaining the telephone system to the mayor, Counciller R. Dutton and Mr Peter Smithers MP in August 1956.

Some of the staff at Brazil's food factory in Winnall in January 1957.

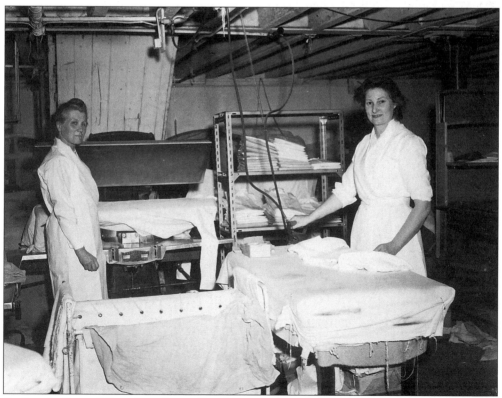

Staff at the Snow White Laundry in Chesil Street, 1956.

Staff at the Winchester boat builders Trowbridge and Son are seen here working in their small factory at No.59 North Walls in 1967.

The interior of Woolworth's store in the High Street, crowded with shoppers in November 1957.

Inside the Winchester Wimpy Bar at No.2 Jewry Street in 1961.

Mr Page making bricks at Colden Common brick works in 1967.

Winchester traffic wardens - who were not too unpopular - leaving the police station in 1970 to start another day. From left to right: Dave Lever, Graham Goodwin, John Wheeler, Len Bumstead, Eric Hewitt and Fred Mitten.

Traffic warden Mary Brown - doing what she was paid to do - in Stockbridge Road in 1972.

Police Constable R. Benson was one of the last constables to leave the old police station in the Guildhall before it closed and moved to the new station in North Walls.

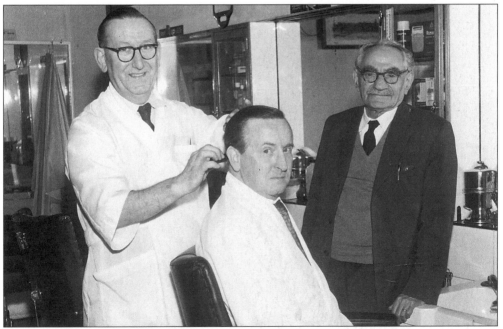

Mr Joe Stone started his gent's hairdressing business in a small shop at the rear of the George Hotel and then moved to No.47 Jewry Street, until he was forced to move to St Thomas Street because of a compulsory purchase order. He also had another shop in Parchment Street, where Bert Arthur was made manager. Seen here with Joe Stone are Bert Arthur and his assistant, Bill Nash in 1968.

Members of Hampshire County Council stand on the steps by the Law Courts in 1982.

Members of Winchester City Council in the Guildhall on 8 November 1973.

The ladies' darts team at the Volunteer Inn, North View, with the cup they won in September 1958.

Members of the Winchester Photographic Society at the Cadena Cafe in 1960.

Members of Class I at St Bartholomew's Hyde School in 1926/27 with their headmaster, Mr Bill Peters.

The Third Form at St Bartholomew's Hyde School in 1927 with their teacher, Mr Cyril Racket.

Mums from Brackenlee with their babes at a get together in 1955 at the popular Shawford nursing home.

Photographer Bob Pendriegh looks after these happy children at one of Winchester Photographic Society's outings, *c.* 1962. Andrew Sollars is on the left, Roberta Sollars is in the centre with Sarah Pendreigh on the right. Andrew now runs the Sollars' photographic business and Sarah runs that of the Pendreigh's.

A group of children from Dr Barnados at the Odeon cinema, Winchester, in April 1965.

It's back to school after the summer holidays for these six little charmers on 1 September 1955.

A classroom in St Peter's Roman Catholic School, Gordon Road, 1956.

Western School netball team 1959/1960, with their teacher Mrs Mary Ogier.

All Saints' School football team were the winners of the 1956/57 Junior Schools Trophy. On the left is their headmaster, Mr Lewington, and on the right is Mr Paice, the deputy head.

Stanmore School football team in 1957.

Stanmore School football team were the proud winners of the Junior Schools Trophy in 1961.

St Peter's School netball team in 1966.

73

Western School athletics team in 1965.

Western School swimming team with trophies and the Mayor of Winchester, Councillor H.C. Bones in 1962.

Four
Royal Visits

Queen Elizabeth II with the Mayor of Winchester Mrs F.S. Thackeray and school children at Wolvesey playing fields, during her official visit to Winchester City and later, to St Cross for the bicentenary parade of the Royal Green Jackets on 25 May 1955.

The Queen with Lt Col the Hon Martin Charteris and General B.J. Majendie in the Royal Green Jackets Museum before going to St Cross for the bicentenary parade in May 1955.

Wintonians on and around the City Butter Cross wait to cheer the Queen as she passes by during her visit to the city on 25 May 1955.

The Queen opens Butser Country Park on the A3 near Petersfield. Here she is seen walking around one of the many exhibits.

Ad Portas ceremony at Winchester College on 19 May 1982. The Queen greets the Prefect of Hall, Mr M.D.E. Jackson after the ceremony before the whole school. She is accompanied by the headmaster, Mr J.L. Thorne MA.

Local people greet the Queen as she walks through Kingsgate Street with the headmaster Mr John Thorne MA and the warden, Lord Aldington, on 19 May 1982.

The Queen, sitting in the centre with the headmaster, John Thorne, is entertained by a short play in the Queen Elizabeth II Theatre during her visit to Winchester College on 19 May 1982.

The royal visit to Winchester Cathedral on 12 April 1979 when the Queen distributed Maundy money to senior citizens.

The same Maundy service. After the ceremoney the Queen and the Duke of Edinburgh pose for a photograph with Bishop J. Taylor, Dean M. Stancliffe, Revd Manisty the Queen's Chaplain and four local school children.

The Duke of Gloucester talks to residents of St John's South during his visit to Winchester in 1972.

Lord Mountbatten of Burma was the guest of honour at the Winchester branch of the Royal Marines Association Annual Dinner in 1966. He is seen here with the Mayor of Winchester, Councillor and Mrs G. Smith, the Chief Constable, Sir Douglas and Lady Osman, Major B.W. de Courcey Ireland and other guests.

Five

City Streets

The Cathedral from St Giles' Hill with the spires of Christ church on the distant left and St Thomas's on the right, c. 1970.

The High Street from St Giles' Hill with the Guildhall in the Broadway and the Hampshire County Council buildings in the background, *c.* 1970.

A view of Wolvesey Palace, the Bishop of Winchester's residence, and the college with Stanmore in the distance, in 1970.

Bridge Street from St John's South tower, with the City Bridge over the River Itchen, *c.* 1972.

Eastgate Street from St John's South tower in 1972.

Seen here in August 1962 is the Co-op Bakery in Eastgate Street, formerly the Lion Brewery.

A view from the roof of the Co-op Bakery looking towards Lawn Street and Boundary Street, with Tagart's saw mills in the centre foreground, April 1961.

84

Lawn Street from Union Street in 1955.

Union Street in 1955 with two public houses. The Waggon and Horses is evident on the right and on the left by the milk lorry is the Bird in Hand.

Cottages being demolished in North Walls for the building of the new police station in 1958.

Moorside Motor Works with the proprietor, Mr C. Hurst, in 1958.

The Waggon & Horses on the corner of Union Street and Lower Brook Street in 1967. It stands alone after the demolition of the houses in Union Street.

Carhart's general store in Lower Brook Street. This house was the scene of a murder during the process of a robbery in 1963.

Demolition of houses in Lower Brook Street in 1960.

Silver Hill as it was, with Ron Stanbrook's shop and the rear of Dick's Ltd electrical business in 1968.

The north side of Silver Hill before demolition in 1968.

Trinity School, viewed from Middle Brook Street in 1965.

This building at Nos 81-83 Middle Brook Street was known locally as 'Pinhead Castle' in 1961.

View from the roof of the Ritz cinema looking south east in 1961.

The drama of a fire at the rear of the International Stores. This view from 1970 overlooks the central car park and the Ritz cinema.

The hustle and bustle of the WI market on the site of the demolished Victoria Inn and the site of future shops in Kings Walk and the new General Post Office in Middle Brook Street, in 1971.

Looking down St Georges Street after the demolition of the George Hotel in 1957.

St Georges Street in 1958, taken from Barclays Bank with the Red Triangle Boys Club clearly visible.

St Georges Street in 1961 before the Casson Block was built.

The corner of Parchment Street in 1960 before the Casson Block was built, showing the corner bakery which was once owned by the Portsmouth family and later by Pragnells, who moved from the Broadway.

Parchment Street south from St Georges Street in 1963, showing the shops of George Smith, W.G. Symes & Son and W. Prall.

Milner's camera shop and Harrington's book shop in Parchment Street in 1971.

The Post Office Tavern with Joe Stone's barbers shop and D.R. Hornsey's wool shop, Parchment Street, November 1955.

H. Baker's shoe repair shop at No.8 Parchment Street in 1959.

The new Barclays Bank viewed from the High Street in 1966.

Jewry Street shops viewed from the roof of Barclays Bank in 1958.

Blanchard's and Hayne's shops in Jewry Street in 1965.

The Royal Theatre and adjacent shops in Jewry Street in 1979.

Hyde Street S.C.A.T.S. and houses in 1956, now demolished and part of offices and Ford car dealers, Evans Halshaw.

Andover Road at a busy time of day with early morning traffic in 1957.

Station Hill and Stockbridge Road, with the Carfax Hotel on the left in 1956, before demolition.

The Carfax Hotel corner of Sussex Street and Station Hill in 1957.

Andover Road shops from the Albion to the Misses Halls' wool shop in 1972.

Master bricklayer Mr Len Houghton (left) with colleagues in 1978 beside the wall of the new Department of the Environment offices in Andover Road. The wall was built with graffiti bricks inscribed by school children of the city.

Andover Road cottages before demolition in 1960.

The Hampshire Police headquarters viewed across the Fulflood area in 1969.

Winchester Prison from the same spot, also in 1969.

Lord Mountbatten at Winchester Prison with a Home Office committee in 1966.

The main entrance to Winchester Prison in 1963 before the Romsey Road access was closed.

The Volunteer Inn, North View, by the old Western School in 1971. The inn is now a private residence.

The County Arms in Romsey Road on the corner of Queens Road in 1968.

The Gate Lodge in 1968 at the Royal Hampshire County Hospital, sadly now demolished.

Sir George Cooper with hospital staff at the opening of the new lift in the nurses' Nightingale Home in 1955.

The demolition of the officers mess in Peninsular Barracks in 1962.

Demolition of part of the Royal Hampshire Regiment's barracks on St James Lane, March 1958.

106

Jack and Pat Moreton by
their St Swithuns Street
works in 1964.

A flooded Kingsgate in 1955.

The College Cottage at the entrance to the Meadows in 1960.

A view taken in the Meadows of St Catherine's Hill over the River Itchen in 1966; the view does not now exist owing to the growth of trees and foliage in the background.

Temporary accommodation in the valley at Stanmore in 1970 whilst council houses were being modernised.

Demolition of the chimney stack at the Garnier Road pumping station in 1978.

This GWR engine, the *City of Truro*, seen here at Chesil station in 1963, was the first steam train to exceed 100 mph.

King Alfred College students in period dress at Chesil station celebrate 100 years of the Great Western Railway in 1963.

It is 1968 and Chesil station is now closed, with the track removed. However, the footbridge leading to St Giles' Hill is still in existence and open to the public.

The Chesil line in 1968, looking south from the station.

The footbridge over the line at the old goods yard in Bar End in 1968, with St Catherine's Hill in the background.

Workmen cutting away the iron bridge at Hockley in 1967.

The viaduct at Hockley in 1962, which is still standing.

A view over the old Winchester bypass from St Catherine's Hill, between Hockley and Bar End in 1978. The tunnel at the centre provided access from the canal towpath to the hill before the closure of the by-pass and after the opening of the completed M3.

Chesil Street in 1961 showing the allotments, where there is now a large car park.

The Blue Boar inn in St Johns Street after restoration in 1971; it is now a private residence.

Jack Schrier, metal sculptor, in Bridge Street, c. 1970.

St Johns Street in 1968.

St John's church from Water Lane in 1956.

Chester Road in 1972.

116

Children playing with snow dumped in the River Itchen at Water Lane, with Durngate House and Mill in the background, *c.* 1963.

Durngate Mill in 1967. The road is now a footpath.

The Mill House at Durngate in 1967, with millstones in the foreground from the demolished mill.

An old sluice gate in Eastgate Street, used in the past to control one of the many streams passing through and under the city in 1960.

The new bridge over the River Itchen in Water Lane, the part of the river which flows through the city in which the public can fish - with a license.

Fire broke out at the headquarters of Currys at Worthy Park in February 1975. Local firemen tackle the fire to bring it under control.

Six

Military and More

The 60th Rifles the Kings Royal Rifle Corps marching down the High Street in 1946.

The Royal Army Pay Corps received the Freedom of the City of Winchester in 1966. The Freedom Casket was paraded between the lines at a ceremony in the Broadway.

The Mayor of Winchester, Councillor Mrs P.A.T. Lowden, inspects units of the Royal Navy from HMS *Ariel*, Worthy Down, for the Queen's Birthday Parade in 1959.

The Royal Navy from HMS *Ariel*, Worthy Down, hand the Key of the Gate to the Royal Army Pay Corps after the takeover of the camp in May 1965.

An old grain store at the Manor House, Chilcombe, 1969.

The RDC litter patrol cleaning up Farley Mount in 1965.

The cottage which was demolished at the British Red Cross Society headquarters at Weeke, on the Stockbridge Road, for road widening.

Archbishop King lying in state at St Peter's Roman Catholic church in Jewry Street, March 1965.

Avington church in 1959, which has the only known barrel organ in any Hampshire church.

Otterbourne's old church in Kiln Lane, photographed in February 1970, no longer stands on the site.

Hursley church with a spire in 1959, before it was removed.

The Roman paving now in Winchester City Museum is seen here in 1969 being lifted from the site of the Roman Villa in Westwood, Sparsholt.

Temple Valley service station, Morn Hill, Alresford Road, Chilcomb, as it was in 1964.

Living in the countryside has its advantages - as the author found out to his pleasure in 1975.

A flotilla of swans cruising down the river in North Walls recreation ground, 1997.